9/95

Everything You Need To Know About

CODEPENDENCY

Unhealthy family relationships may lead to feelings of loneliness and low self-esteem.

• THE NEED TO KNOW LIBRARY •

Everything You Need To Know About

CODEPENDENCY

Al Septien

THE ROSEN PUBLISHING GROUP, INC.
NEW YORK

Published in 1993 by The Rosen Publishing Group, Inc.
29 East 21st Street, New York, NY 10010

First Edition
Copyright © 1993 by The Rosen Publishing Group, Inc.

Manufactured in the United States of America.

Library of Congress Cataloging-in-Publication Data

Septien, Al.
    Everything you need to know about codependency / Al Septien —
1st ed.
      p.   cm. — (The Need to know library)
    Includes bibliographical references and index.
    Summary: Discusses the unhealthy relationships that exist in some families and how to break the cycle of codependency.
    ISBN 0-8239-1527-1
    1. Codependency—Juvenile literature. [1. Codependency.
2. Interpersonal relations. 3. Family life.] I. Title.
RC669.5.C63S47 1993
616.86—dc20   93-17380
                                                   CIP
                                                   AC

Contents

Introduction

All of us need other people. In relationships that are considered healthy, people share love, concern, and respect for one another. There is an equal amount of give-and-take—an *interdependence*. People help each other but remain individuals. They have their own feelings and opinions. They make their own decisions and take responsibility for their actions.

In some unhealthy relationships, people seem unwilling or unable to take care of themselves. They may be out of touch with their own feelings and needs. They have little self-esteem. The only way they can feel good about themselves is by fulfilling the expectations of others. This is *codependency* at work.

Codependency is a complex disorder that thrives in unhealthy relationships. Codependency has identifiable symptoms and follows certain patterns of behavior. A person suffering from codependency is called a *codependent*. Codependents become so focused on others that they can "lose" themselves. Personal boundaries (limits set between yourself and others) become confused. If not treated, codependency can result in destructive behavior, depression, anxiety, physical illness, or even death.

How do you become codependent? How do you know if you are codependent? What should you do if you recognize codependent behavior in yourself? In your family? You can find the answers to these and other questions about codependency by reading this book. It is important to be aware of your own behavior. It is important to understand *why* you act as you do.

If you are unhappy with yourself and your life, you may be caught in the trap of codependency. But you can free yourself. Help is available. You can learn how to make changes in yourself and in the way you deal with others. You can learn to love yourself and take control of your life.

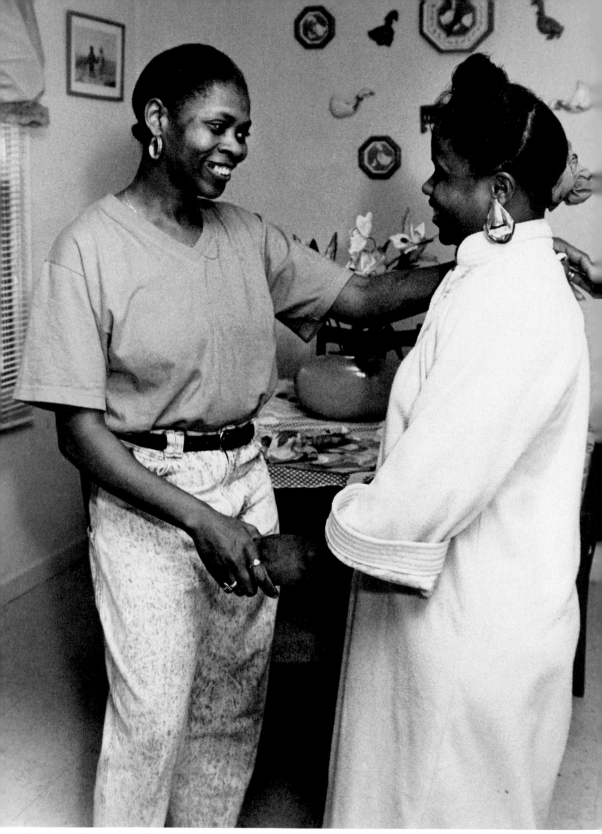

Parental approval is important for healthy emotional development.

Chapter 1

What Is Codependency?

Codependency is a problem of relationships. It has many forms and expressions. Codependents, however, do have things in common. Most codependents have not learned how to love *themselves* or figure out what *they* need. Therefore, they usually develop poor relationships. A popular song a few years ago expressed a similar idea, "I can't be right for somebody else if I'm not right for me."

Codependents have such low self-esteem that they live their lives according to what others think of them. They need to be well thought of and important to other people. They try too hard to meet the needs of others. Often codependents act as "caretakers," doing for another person what that person is able to do for himself or herself. At other times codependents act as "rescuers," trying to save someone from the rightful consequences of his or her behavior.

It's hard work always trying to meet the expectations of others. And when your feelings about yourself depend upon the behavior of others, you set yourself up for failure. In the later stages of codependency, codependents feel used and resentful. They become confused and fearful of losing all control in their world. Without counseling, the helplessness they feel may bring on depression, sickness, or thoughts of suicide.

Does This Sound Like You?

Look at the list below. Can you relate to any of these feelings? Keep in mind how often you feel this way (once in a while, sometimes, most of the time, always).

- I feel like a failure.
- I can't make friends.
- I have a lot of friends, but none of them are close.
- When people say nice things about me, I don't believe them.
- I have a hard time expressing my feelings.
- I'm afraid of losing my friends.
- My decisions are wrong.
- I let others make all my decisions.
- I'm afraid people won't like me.
- It's better to be a giver than a taker.

- If you get close to people, you'll just get hurt.
- Nobody cares about me.
- I get angry at people all of a sudden for no reason.
- When I'm angry, I take it out on the wrong person.
- I must make other people happy, even if I'm not happy.
- I hate telling others how I really feel.
- I blame myself when things go wrong.
- If I don't agree with people, I'm afraid they won't like me.
- I let somebody else lead the conversation. I'm afraid of saying something stupid.
- Arguing makes me uncomfortable.
- I do what someone else wants. I have no opinion of my own.
- I feel responsible for solving other people's problems.

If you always feel unsure of yourself and unable to make your own decisions, you may be hooked on codependent behavior. It is normal to feel uncertain and uncomfortable from time to time. And it is okay to want to please others. But if you feel that way most of the time and allow others to take advantage of you, then you need help.

You may hear people say that these feelings are just a phase that you're going through. But that is not necessarily true. It is not normal if you always feel defeated. It is not just a phase to feel insecure,

angry, fearful, guilty, or depressed all the time.
Having these feelings is not wrong, but it is a warn-
ing that you are losing control. And losing control
is not healthy.

Codependency keeps you from enjoying life. It
discourages you from setting your own goals. It
prevents you from reaching your full potential.
Codependency makes it difficult to form positive
relationships. It keeps you weak by reinforcing
negative thoughts about yourself.

Codependency and Addiction

*Anja came home from school and found her
mother passed out in the living room. She was drunk
again. Anja wanted to help. She began to clean up
the mess her mother had made. After she finished,
Anja went upstairs to do her homework. Later she
relaxed by listening to a new CD. When Anja's
mother woke up, she yelled at Anja for being lazy and
wasting time. Anja just sat there quietly. She was
too hurt to defend herself and explain things to her
mother.*

*When Anja went downstairs later to fix dinner,
her mother screamed at her again. Her mother
wanted another beer in the living room. Anja knew
that would only make her mother worse, but she did
as she was told. She tried to make her mother happy.
Anja watched sadly as her mother drank and fell
back on the couch. Nothing Anja did was ever right.
At least, that's the way it felt to her.*

Some teens need approval from a parent and will take on more than their share of responsibility to get it.

Doctors first recognized codependency when they were working with the families of *alcoholics*. Alcoholics are people who are addicted to alcohol. They have no control over their drinking. They continue drinking even though they know it is hurting them and others. Their disease is called *alcoholism*.

When doctors studied alcoholics, they found a disorder in the family members of the alcoholic as well. Look at the example of Anja and her mother.

Anja's mother suffers from alcoholism. When she drinks, she treats Anja badly. She cannot provide the love, care, and respect that Anja needs from the mother-daughter relationship. Anja feels trapped. She loves her mother and wants to help her. But when Anja tries to lend a hand around the house, her mother yells. If Anja brings her mother another beer, her mother becomes drunker and meaner. Anya feels that nothing she ever does is right.

Anja is caught in a *codependent relationship* with her mother. As an alcoholic, Anja's mother doesn't admit that she has a problem. She neglects her responsibilities as a mother. She blames others for the way she acts. Anja's mother wants and relies only on alcohol. She is dependent on her drinking.

Anja is dependent on her mother. She needs her mother's love and approval. Anja feels guilty and confused about her mother's drinking. She wonders why her mother continues to drink. She always worries about her mother. Anja may feel that if only she were a better daughter, maybe her mother would stop drinking. She is affected in many ways by her mother's chemical dependency, the need to drink. Anja is codependent.

Codependency itself is considered an addiction. People who have addictions are devoted to something or some kind of behavior that hurts them. They cannot stop themselves. They are called addicts. Codependents are "addicted" to people in a way that is harmful to them.

What Some Experts Say

Doctors have learned that you don't have to live with an alcoholic (or any other substance abuser) to become codependent. Many life experiences bring on this behavior disorder. Some of these are discussed in the chapters that follow.

It is important to remember that you do not have to accept codependent behavior in yourself or in the people you care about. There are many trained professionals who treat codependent people. Many have already been helped. There are proven ways to stop codependency from running your life. You can learn to be happy if you ask for the help you need.

Chapter 2

What Does Codependency Feel Like?

There are eight areas of codependent behavior. It is important to remember that most of these feelings are felt by everyone at some time. The difference is that codependents feel them *most* of the time, and the feelings control their behavior.

"I'm Not Good Enough"—Low Self-Esteem

The value and respect that each person feels for himself or herself is known as *self-esteem*. Codependents don't recognize their own value as human beings. They suffer from low self-esteem. No matter what they do, codependents feel it's not enough. They feel they are not as good as others.

In a healthy family, all members are respected and appreciated for their contributions.

Some codependents try to cover up their low self-esteem. They like to point out the "faults" in other people to make themselves look better.

"I'll Do Whatever You Want" —Other-Esteem

In place of self-esteem, codependents have *other-esteem*. They look to other people to judge how they should feel about themselves. Codependents can be happy only when others are happy with them. They become "people pleasers."

It is not uncommon to want your friends and family to be pleased with you. But codependents fear being abandoned if their friends or families are not happy. Codependents think that what others are feeling is their fault. So codependents will do anything to please others.

"Too Much or Not at All"—Going to Extremes

Codependents relate to other people in extremes. There's never a healthy give-and-take in their relationships. They either give too much or not at all.

As people pleasers, codependents "give till it hurts." They do favors for everyone. They go out of their way to take on responsibilities. Sometimes they even do things that are harmful to themselves.

Eventually, the codependent burns out. He or she feels used and resentful and gives up trying to please. When this happens, codependents pull away from other people altogether. They have nothing left to give.

Children often blame themselves when their parents don't get along.

In a codependent relationship, a child may be expected to do things for a parent that a parent could and should do for himself or herself.

"I Don't Feel Anything"—Denying True Feelings

Codependents are often confused about how they really feel. Their only concern is how others feel about them. While codependents seem happy on the outside, their true feelings may be eating away at them inside.

"I Can Make You Think the Way I Want"—Control and Manipulation of Others

Codependents lose control over their own feelings and needs. But codependents are experts at trying to control and manipulate others. They often play *"communication games."*

"Pity Me." Codependents play the martyr, so that others feel sorry for them.

"You Should Know How I Feel." Codependents don't express themselves, yet they get angry at others for not understanding them.

"Forgive Me." To avoid problems, codependents apologize for everything—even when they haven't done anything wrong.

"Let's Talk about Something Else." Codependents want to avoid confrontation. When an uncomfortable topic is brought up, codependents try to change the subject .

"Did You Hear What They Said?" Codependents won't tell you what they want directly. They're afraid of saying something that won't please. When they need to make a point, they make it sound as if they are expressing the opinion of another.

"You're Right, I'm Wrong." To make themselves seem more agreeable, codependents go along with almost anything you say.

By using these games, codependents free themselves from the responsibility of communicating. They don't tell or show their true feelings. They try to manipulate others to gain self-esteem. They want to control how others feel so they can feel good about themselves. But it doesn't work. No one can really control what others feel.

"Shoo, Don't Bother Me"—Problems with Getting Close

Codependents need other people. They are addicted to people. But they can't get too close. They're afraid of *intimacy*. They do not show their true feelings or let people know what they are really like because they're afraid people won't like them.

Codependents never focus on the positive side of a relationship. Instead, they worry about possible disappointment and being hurt. They fear being "dumped" or abandoned, so they keep others at a safe distance.

"I Just Can't Do It"—Powerlessness

Codependents don't trust their own judgment. They usually let others decide how they should feel or act. Sometimes they do what they think others want them to do. Since they're looking *outside* of themselves for how they should feel, they have no

Trying to be perfect at school and at home can create a great deal of pressure.

control over their own feelings. This can lead to frustration, anger, depression, and, if not treated, suicide.

"I Get By with a Little Help"—Addictions and Compulsions

Codependents often feel empty inside. They may look for relief in harmful ways. They can become addicted to cigarettes, alcohol, or other drugs. They may feel driven to excess in some activities, such as watching TV or shopping. Over-eating, overwork, and perfectionism (only the best) are also common codependent behaviors.

Our attitudes about ourselves and other family members are formed at an early age.

Chapter 3

How Did I Become Codependent?

You did not choose the color of your hair or eyes when you were born. Likewise, you did not choose your family. *Codependents are born into families in which codependency is a normal way of life*. You *learned* to be codependent from your family. People born into codependent families use the same behavior that their families use to survive.

Healthy Families

Your family has the greatest influence on you. It helps to shape the kind of person you become, and how you feel about yourself. A healthy family fills certain needs for its members:

- the need to be loved and accepted
- the need to feel safe and secure
- the need to express yourself

- the need for guidance, support, and encour-
  agement
- the need for privacy.

No family is perfect. All families have problems. Family members disagree. That's normal. But when families care about each other and meet the basic needs of their members (love, support, trust), they provide a healthy environment. Children have a chance to grow and develop into confident, happy, and responsible adults.

Unhealthy Families

Some families do not relate to each other in positive ways. Their interaction does not provide a healthy environment for their members. These are called *dysfunctional* families.

Many life situations can create dysfunctional families. Families that must deal with addictions, codependent parents, abuse, family secrets, and major stress are all at risk. Codependency begins in the dysfunctional family. In the following stories, try to identify the feelings of the family members. Perhaps you can see the beginning of codependent behavior.

Steven's father is abusive toward Steven's mother. Sometimes he comes home angry after a bad day at work. He finds some reason to yell at his wife. When she tries to defend herself, he gets violent. Last week, Steven's father gave his wife a black eye.

The rest of the family is scared. Steven's father told the kids that he was head of the house, he made the rules. Steven is the oldest child. He is almost 12. Steven feels guilty that he can't protect his mother.

Michael's father played varsity football in college. His two older brothers are also very good athletes. But Michael is not interested in sports. He does not enjoy competition. His dad pushes him to play sports, but Michael would rather do other things. His dad calls him "the nerd of the family."

Carol comes from a loving family. They are well known in the community. But they have a secret. Carol's older sister, Janet, is a lesbian. Carol's parents are embarrassed and angry about their daughter's homosexuality. Her mother doesn't allow talk of it in the house. Carol doesn't know who is right or wrong; she just does as she is told.

Serious family problems can cause confusion. Members have mixed feelings and may lose confidence in the family unit, and in themselves. As fear, guilt, blame, and low self-esteem take hold, codependent behavior thrives.

Dysfunctional Families at Work

Members of dysfunctional families don't always know that they are codependent. They may just *feel* that something is not right. Since the family refuses to talk about its problem, family members learn to keep their feelings hidden and pretend that all is well. When communication is not open and honest, codependency gets worse.

Dysfunctional families often have unspoken rules for their members. Do any of the following rules apply to you and your family?

"All we need is our family." Dysfunctional families believe they can solve their own problems. Anyone trying to help from the outside is a threat.

"Don't talk outside the family." In the dysfunctional family, you're discouraged to discuss "family matters" outside the home. This can be particularly harmful if the "family matter" is abuse or addiction.

"You shouldn't feel like that." Family members are told to hide their feelings. Members are warned not to tell family secrets because it will split up the family.

"Watch your back!" Dysfunctional families feel that everyone else is wrong. You are warned not to trust others because you'll only be hurt.

"It's not that way at all." Family members are deceived. They are led to believe that there are no problems in the home. The message is to deny what's really going on. The important thing is for the family to seem perfect.

"Do it our way or leave!" Dysfunctional family members believe that if they make waves by telling the truth or suggesting that there's a problem, they are being disloyal to their family. They believe that they won't be loved.

Even when a teen must admit that a parent has a drinking problem, he or she may not be able to confront the parent directly about it.

"Shame, shame!" How dare you suggest that the family is not perfect! How dare you complain about what the family expects of you! In a dysfunctional family, you're always made to feel ashamed of what you do or say.

"Never mind you, help me." Since the dysfunctional family is such a mess, it constantly calls on you for help. You are required to put your own needs and feelings aside. You must do it "for the good of the family."

Roles in the Codependent Family

In codependent families, each member assumes a role with certain predictable patterns. Playing out these "characters" or "jobs" keeps the family trapped in the problem.

The Problem. In an alcoholic or drug-addicted family, "the Problem" is the person who has the addiction. In a family suffering from physical, emotional, or sexual abuse, it is the abuser.

The Hero. This is usually the spouse or one of the older children. The hero may feel responsible somehow for the family's problem. He or she is the one who tries to keep the family together at all costs.

The Lost Child. Also called the *withdrawn* or *silent child*, this member tries to hide from the family problems. He or she can not deal with what is going on and prefers his or her own quiet thoughts. The lost child is often alone.

The Scapegoat. This family member is some-times also "the Problem." He or she always gets into trouble. This *rebel* or *delinquent* is looking for attention and love.

The Comic. This family member may be the most scared. He or she helps the others to cope by making them laugh. It keeps them from dealing with the real problems that are going on in the family.

Dysfunctional families rarely heal themselves. To become healthy, family members must talk about their problems and how they really feel. If you recognize codependent behavior in yourself, you are ready to step outside your family and get help. You may not be able to change your family situation. But professional counseling can help you to feel better about yourself. You can protect your-self from any destructive behavior that you learned as a child.

Children need to know that they are loved even when they displease their parents.

Chapter 4

Living in Shame

e first feel *shame* as children. Shame is a
feeling of disgrace. When our parents scold us for
doing something wrong, we know they are unhappy with us. We may feel unloved. We may
worry that our parents will leave us.

A good parent reassures a child that he or she is
only angry at what the child did. The parent com-
forts the child's fear of being abandoned and lets
the child know that he or she is still loved. A good
parent shows the child how to make up for the
wrongdoing and forgives him or her.

In dysfunctional families, the parents deal with
their children differently. Forgiveness is rare.
Children learn to feel shame as a way of life.

Children in a dysfunctional family are not told that they simply made a mistake (guilt). They are told that they *are* the mistake (shame). Dysfunctional parents don't help their children see their errors. Instead, the children are told that they can't do anything right.

The parents in dysfunctional families may shame their children for several reasons:

- The parents don't know any better. They think shame is just a form of discipline.
- Their own parents may have shamed them. They pass on what they learned.
- The parents may confuse self-esteem with vanity (excessive pride). In some cultures and religions, feeling good about yourself is played down.

When children grow up feeling shamed over and over, they lose faith in themselves. They are easy victims of codependency. After all, how can you do anything right if you're the mistake?

Outside the Dysfunctional Family

When you come from a dysfunctional family, you live in shame and fear. You may be unfamiliar with normal behavior. Codependents expect the rest of the world to treat them as they have been treated at home.

To protect themselves, codependents build up defenses. They are afraid that they will be shamed

Living in a dysfunctional family can be painful and confusing.

for what they feel. Codependents deny their feelings and emotions in one of several ways.

"The Water Balloon"—Stuffing Feelings

Afraid of feelings that might cause trouble,
codependents "stuff" their feelings inside. Unfortu-
nately, feelings do not disappear. When you fill a
balloon with water, it reaches a point at which it can
take no more. The person who stuffs feelings also
reaches a limit. Once the limit is crossed, the person breaks and the stuffed emotions pour out.

Stuffed feelings come out at unexpected times.
Even a casual remark can trigger the powerful
emotions that are held inside.

"You Won't Feel a Thing"—Numbness

Codependents deny their feelings. Over time
they may become *numb*. They forget how to feel.

Doctors have found that denying emotions can
harm you physically. Feeling numb does not mean
that your natural emotions have gone away. Feelings that are not dealt with can cause heart disease,
high blood pressure, asthma, migraine headaches,
and other illnesses.

"The Magnet"—Taking on the Feelings of Others

When codependents are faced with a situation
that makes them uneasy, they look to others to
supply feelings. Like a magnet, they pick up the
emotions and opinions of others. In this way, they
avoid disagreement and try to please others.

"Second Guessing"—Feeling What You Think Others Want You to Feel

Codependents won't express what they are feeling. Instead, they show the emotion that they *think* others expect. How do codependents know what others expect? *They don't.* They're only guessing.

These "games" that codependents play with their feelings can be dangerous. Codependents are not being honest with themselves. They are cheating themselves of their right to "feel." In the advanced stages of their disease, codependents may give in to despair. Without proper treatment, codependents may see suicide as the only way to relieve their emotional pain.

All teens need time for fun and play.

Chapter 5

The "Kid Inside"

*E*loise lives with her father and her grandmother. Her mother died two years ago. It's hard to believe that Eloise is only 12. She acts like an adult.

Eloise is responsible at school and at home. Her assignments are always in on time. Her desk is neat, and her locker is organized. After school Eloise helps other students with their homework.

But Eloise never has fun. When she is invited to go places with friends, she politely refuses by making up some excuse. She spends her time caring for her grandmother and cleaning the house. Up in her room, she often feels sad and lonely.

Eloise loves her family. She likes to make them happy. But she doesn't understand why she feels so bad. Everyone praises her for being so grown-up.

Eloise's family has become dysfunctional. Since the death of her mother, Eloise has had an unfair amount of responsibility at home. Her family does not meet her needs to grow in a healthy way. She has learned to put her own needs aside. Eloise is playing the role of "the Hero." She feels responsible to keep the family together. Eloise is codependent.

Codependents often act grown-up, but they pay for it in other ways. They lose touch with the more innocent, playful side that lives in every person. This side is honest. It only knows how to feel, see, and react truthfully. Codependents lose touch with what we will call the *"Kid Inside."*

The Kid Inside is also known as your *true self*, the real you. It does not know how to cover up emotions. It's the voice inside that wants to speak out. It has the natural reactions that you deny. The Kid Inside is "squashed" by codependency.

Learning to Hold Back

In dysfunctional families the Kid Inside is silenced. Sometimes the parents are directly to blame. For example, if you speak your mind and are told to shut up, if you point out a family problem and are told that you are imagining things, or if you express your feelings and are teased, then you are learning to keep the Kid Inside quiet. Your family is making it clear that to be accepted, you must hide your true self.

Sometimes kids like Eloise get an unspoken message. "This family is okay." "We don't need anyone else." "Doing for the good of the family will make you happy." Here, too, you tell your true self to stop feeling, talking, and reacting. You become careful of everything you say or do. As a result, your Kid Inside suffers.

Children need to learn certain things as they grow. These lessons are important in order for them to develop into happy, healthy adults. They must learn to:

- like themselves
- know who they are
- trust and relate to others
- experience life on their own
- admit their feelings and opinions
- take care of themselves
- stand up for what they believe
- enjoy life.

Codependents miss these childhood life lessons. The Kid Inside is trapped. The Kid Inside does not go away, but emotionally, it stops growing.

To recover from codependency you must learn to know your Kid Inside better. In Chapter 7 there are some mental exercises to help you get started. The Kid Inside needs to "play." It needs to express who you really are. Codependents who connect with their Kid Inside have a chance to live a fuller, happier life.

If parents and children don't talk about their feelings, there can't be true understanding.

Chapter 6

New Lessons to Learn

Now that you know about the Kid Inside (your true self), it's time to start listening to it. You can teach yourself to relate to yourself and others without the cover of codependency. There are four important areas to work on.

Feelings

Mario's parents hardly ever fought. Mario was shocked to learn that they were getting a divorce. He watched sadly as his father moved out. Mario told his dad that he understood.

But inside, Mario didn't understand. He felt angry and confused. He blamed himself. Maybe if he hadn't been born, his parents would still love each other and be together.

The divorce seemed quiet and friendly. No one really talked about it. Mario kept his feelings to himself. He tried to go along with the changes in his life. He thought that was what his parents wanted. As months passed, Mario started to skip classes and let his grades slip. He quit the swim team and spent most of his time alone at home.

Mario's teacher noticed the change in him. She asked if anything was wrong at home. Mario said no and told his teacher to mind her own business. He stomped out of her office and slammed the door.

Mario had strong feelings about his parents' divorce. He was sad that they had split up. He felt hurt that no one seemed to care how he felt. Mostly, he was angry that his parents never told him *why* they got divorced.

But Mario stuffed his feelings, instead of dealing with them. He never asked his parents to explain. He never told them honestly how he felt. (He didn't let the Kid Inside express itself!) As time passed, Mario's emotions began to show up in destructive ways.

To change codependent behavior, you must first "claim" your own feelings. You have a right to feel any way you want. Remember that your feelings are not right or wrong. They are not good or bad. They are just natural reactions that come from within. Your Kid Inside needs to experience these emotions openly.

Communicating

Once you start to recognize your true feelings, you need to express them. Sharing your feelings with another person is called *communication*.

If you come from a dysfunctional family, you were not encouraged to express yourself. You must move beyond that silence now. To begin healing from codependency, you must learn to talk about what *you* feel and stop trying only to please others. This can be very scary. Others will not always agree with you. That's okay. It's not wrong or selfish to have your own opinion.

Good communication is important for healthy relationships. When people express themselves honestly, there is a give-and-take between them. No one person takes control. People who have been trapped in codependent behavior for a long time need to develop new communication skills. Here are some helpful hints.

- You don't have to speak up right away in every situation. Some feelings are harder to talk about than others. Take your time. Wait until you feel ready.
- Know what you want to say. Be prepared.
- Say what's on your mind clearly. Try to keep it simple.
- Find the right time and place to express your feelings to another person. Both of you need to be prepared.

- You don't need to express *every* feeling with *every* person. You can decide what emotions to share and with whom.

Communication requires both talking and listening. Codependents often have *selective deafness*. That means that they hear only what they want to hear. Codependents are quick to accept blame and shame. It is hard for them to listen to good things about themselves. But it is important for recovery to be able to accept compliments and thanks. You deserve it. And your self-esteem needs it.

Setting Boundaries

Sacha really liked Jon. She thought he was the best-looking boy in her class. When he asked her out to the movies, Sacha was thrilled.

In the middle of the movie, Jon reached under Sacha's sweater and started to feel her breast. "Relax. It's okay," Jon said. But Sacha felt nervous and uncomfortable. She'd never had a boy do this to her before. Although she liked Jon, she didn't want to be touched in that way. She felt angry that he was taking advantage of her.

But Sacha said nothing. She worried that if she stopped him, Jon might not like her anymore. What if Jon went back to school and told everyone that Sacha was a prude? The other kids would tease her. So she put her feelings aside. She cried later when she was alone in her room.

Talking to a trusted friend or relative can be the first step in sorting out family relationships and personal feelings.

The balance of power in a codependent's relationship is never equal. Sacha, for example, has no control in her relationship with Jon. She gives up her needs to please him. Sacha keeps the voice of her Kid Inside quiet. She does not "listen" to what she is really feeling. She allows Jon to make himself happy at her expense.

Codependents don't see the *boundaries* needed in relationships. Boundaries are natural, healthy emotional separations between people. They help you understand who you are. It is important to know what *you* feel, what *you* need, and what *you* want. You are an individual who needs to make decisions for yourself.

When codependents try to please and second-guess what others want, they blur the boundaries. As a result, they allow people to hurt them. They invite trouble from the bullies and abusers of the world. Like Sacha, they allow others to tell them how to think and feel. They give up their sense of self to gain self-esteem from others. As a result, most codependents are taken advantage of.

Codependents can also "crowd" others when boundaries are not clear. They please people to control how others feel about them. Some codependents become intimate with everyone they meet and make lots of friends. Some codependents like to take care of others. They are always ready to *give* advice. Again, they can overstep boundaries when trying to "fix" other people.

Everyone needs to set boundaries in relationships. These boundaries must be flexible so that
we can allow some people to get close and keep
others at a distance. Boundaries allow us to grow.
They help us make choices. They put us in touch
with our own feelings. They help us to know where
one person stops and where we begin.

Trust

The final step in healing is learning to trust. If
you grew up in a dysfunctional home, you learned
to mistrust your family. More important, you lost
the ability to trust yourself. Even when you saw
your father drinking heavily, your mother insisted
that he wasn't an alcoholic. Maybe you told your
mother that your older brother was sexually abus-
ing you, and she answered, "That's not possible;
your brother loves you."

You may have learned to put up a "wall" around
yourself, making it hard for anyone to get to know
you. As a result, relationships with others may
have been brief and disappointing. With every
disappointment, you learn to mistrust even more.
You make excuses for not having close friends.
Does this sound familiar?

You are not alone. Many codependents need to
relearn how to trust. But it is worth the effort.
Establishing strong, healthy relationships with
others is necessary to human growth. And to get
closer to people, you need to trust again.

There is a middle ground between being addicted to people and not trusting at all. It's called
interdependence. This is the healthy give-and-take,
the sharing, that happens in good, strong relationships. It is the kind of relationship that promotes
trust.

It takes time to build these lasting relationships.
Often codependents get discouraged easily.

In any relationship you need to figure out first
who is *worthy* of your trust. Listen to your Kid
Inside when dealing with people. Now that you
know it's okay to have your own feelings, trust your
instincts You may need help in the beginning.
Talk about trust to your counselor or therapist.
Support groups and peer groups are safe places to
communicate. Even if you misjudge people and get
hurt again, all is not lost. As you understand yourself more, you will be better able to place your
trust in those who deserve it.

Chapter 7

How to Help Yourself

Most codependents need professional help to recover from codependency. There are many self-help support groups that deal with this complex disorder. It's up to you to ask for assistance. Look in the back of this book for information on where to go for help.

But you also can begin your recovery at home. Remember that recovery may be a slow process. You may be dealing with many years of destructive behavior and stuffed feelings.

The Journal

One of the most important tools to help you get started is a *journal*. A journal is a personal daily record, a kind of diary. Each day you write down

your most private thoughts. Remember, *nothing in
your journal is right or wrong*. The notes are your
natural emotions and ideas that you want to express safely. It may feel good at the end of the day
to sort out your feelings.   Be honest. There is no
need to keep secrets anymore. As you heal, you
may begin to express your feelings to others.

Exercises for the Kid Inside

Contacting your Kid Inside is the first job in
understanding your true self. Here too, your
journal can help.

Take some time alone and try to see yourself as
a child. In your journal draw a picture of your Kid
Inside. Try to remember what your feelings were
as a child. Close your eyes and listen to the Kid
Inside. Talk to him. Using your journal again,
write an imaginary conversation with the Kid Inside. Write a letter. Tell him that you love him and
that you're sorry for neglecting him. Have him
write a letter back. Ask him to tell you what he
wants and needs from you. Explain that it's safe for
him to express himself now.

The emotions that you uncover may be very
strong. You may need to set limits. Tell your support group about the exercises you are doing at
home. They can help to direct you.

You may feel silly at first. But this is serious
work. Thousands of codependents of all ages are
following these methods to get to know their true

Journal writing can be a helpful form of expression and a record of growth and change.

Following your own interests and developing your own talents will
help to strengthen self-esteem.

selves. Making friends and being good to that "inner child" is the most important part of curing codependency.

Learning How to Set Boundaries

You may feel close to many people—family, friends, coworkers, or teachers. Make a list of these people in your journal. Now check your *comfort level* with each of them.

Ask yourself the following questions to find out how much at ease you feel with the people on your list. Be honest with your answers.

- Who makes you feel good about yourself?
- Who makes you feel uncomfortable?
- Who knows you the best?
- What kind of things could you share? Any secrets?
- How much would you do for each person?
- What could you ask of each person?
- How close could you get to each person physically?
- Who likes you the way you are? Who tries to change you?

There are no wrong answers. These comfort levels are your personal opinions. You don't have to feel the same about everyone. People are different. You should set flexible boundaries for each relationship based on your comfort level with the person.

Once you have set the boundaries, stick to them when you communicate with the people on your list. Learn to say no politely. Tell people that you still like them or love them, even if you disagree. Be direct with your words, but tell people how you feel. Don't let others speak for you. Learn to be responsible for what you want and need. Likewise, *you* must respect the boundaries of others. Listening is important, too.

You may find that some people refuse to accept your new boundaries. They want to keep their relationship with you the way it was before. If you don't feel strong enough at first to stay within your boundaries around those people, spend less time with them. You don't need to be rude. But you don't have to put yourself in a position that makes you uncomfortable. You have a choice.

Physical or sexual abuse is a total disregard of your comfort levels and boundaries. Abuse of this kind requires immediate assistance. Talk to any responsible adult. Make someone listen.

You can't force others to change. But you can and must help yourself. The road to recovery from codependency starts and ends with you.

Letting Go of the Past

Codependents often need to grieve for the loss of childhood. This is done much the way you would grieve over the death of a loved one. Recovering codependents go through five stages of grief:

Positive relationships with friends provide emotional support and encourage self-confidence.

Denial. Codependents are not easily convinced. They still want to believe that their dysfunctional family is healthy and happy.

Anger. When codependents understand how they were hurt by their childhood experiences, they may feel rage at family members. They are angry at the abuse or neglect they suffered.

Sadness. Later in recovery, codependents are able to hate what happened to them without hating the people who did it. They become sad because they never experienced the happy childhood that they now can imagine.

57

Apathy. Codependents feel drained at this point. They may stop feeling anything for a while. Then new feelings begin to appear. It takes time to sort them out.

Acceptance. Codependents accept that nothing can be done to change their past. They stop hiding from it or fighting it. They become free to take charge of their lives.

The grieving process takes time. It is different for each codependent. You may need professional help to get through it successfully. It's scary, too! After all, you are learning to let go of old, familiar patterns. You are also leaving blame and self-pity behind. You are learning to *take care of yourself*—perhaps for the first time in your life.

Recovering from codependency—whatever it takes— is well worth it. Only then can you restore your self-esteem. Only then can you recognize how valuable you are. Only then can you build a fuller, more satisfying life.

Glossary—*Explaining New Words*

abuse To misuse; to use wrongly.

addiction Dependence on a kind of behavior or a substance that is harmful.

alcoholism A chemical dependence on alcohol.

boundary Emotional separation between people that distinguishes one person's feelings, emotions, choices, and needs from another's.

compulsive behavior Actions based on an irresistible repeated impulse.

dysfunctional family Family that does not operate to meet the needs of all its members in a healthy way.

grief Sadness because of the loss of something (or someone) special.

incest Sexual abuse by a family member.

interdependence Relationship between people in which the balance of power is shared equally, an equal amount of give-and-take.

intimacy Private, familiar, and comfortable closeness between people.

Kid Inside True inner self, the real you.

manipulation Working in an unfair way to make something happen that suits your own needs.

numb Having no feeling.

"other-esteem" Relying on others or outside forces to establish one's own feeling of worth.

rescuer One who tries to prevent another from experiencing the needed consequences of his or her behavior.

self-esteem How you think of yourself, your self-worth.

shame Painful sense of having done something, or being, incurably wrong.

Where to Go for Help

There are many self-help support groups that deal with dysfunctional families and their problems. Your **guidance counselor, social worker,** or **school psychologist** may be able to help you find a group that meets in your area.

You could also look in the Yellow Pages of the phone book under **Mental Health Services, Family Counseling,** or **Psychologists**.

Call or write:

Codependents Anonymous (CODA)
P.O. Box 33577
Phoenix, AZ 85067-3577

National Association of Children of Alcoholics
31706 Pacific Coast Highway
South Laguna, CA 95677
(714) 499-3889

Al-Anon/Alateen Family Group Headquarters
P.O. Box 862, Midtown Station
New York, NY 10018-6106
(212) 302-7240

Families Anonymous
(Families of substance abusers)
P.O. Box 528
Van Nuys, CA 91408

For Further Reading

Beattie, Melody. *Codependent No More.* New York: Harper Collins, 1989.

McFarland, Rhoda. *Drugs and Your Parents*, rev. ed. New York: Rosen Publishing Group, 1993.

Mellody, Pia. *Facing Codependence.* San Francisco: Harper San Francisco, 1989.

Porterfield, Kay Marie. *Coping with Codependency.* New York: Rosen Publishing Group, 1991.

Schaef, Anne Wilson. *Co-Dependence.* San Francisco: Harper San Francisco, 1986.

Thomas, Alicia. *Self-Esteem*, rev.ed. New York: Rosen Publishing Group, 1993.

Index

About the Author
Al Septien is a free-lance writer who has written for a number of media. His one-act play *Birthday Present* is included in an anthology of Latino playwrights. He currently lives in Los Angeles, California.

Photo Credits
Cover photo by Chuck Peterson.
Photo on page 20: Chris Volpe; p. 32: Stuart Rabinowitz; all other photos by Dru Nadler.

Design/Production: Blackbirch Graphics, Inc.